A HOLIDAY BOOK

Thanksgiving

BY LEE WYNDHAM

ILLUSTRATED BY HAZEL HOECKER

GARRARD PUBLISHING COMPANY
CHAMPAIGN, ILLINOIS

For our Janie and Bill—
whose roots reach down
to Elder Brewster and beyond . . .

Holiday Books are edited under
the educational supervision of

Charles E. Johnson, Ed.D.
Associate Professor of Education
University of Illinois

Contents

1
The Two
Mayflowers

In the spring of 1957 a little ship, *Mayflower II*, sailed from Plymouth, England. It was bound for Plymouth, Massachusetts. The ship was a model of the one that brought the Pilgrims to America in 1620. It had been built by the English as a gift to the people of America.

Mayflower II was the same size as the first *Mayflower*. It was 90 feet long and 25 feet wide. It had a few extras that our Pilgrim fathers did not have. There was a generator which made electricity and a two-way radio. There was a wheel for steering instead of a tiller, and a little kitchen.

A crew of 33 sailed the ship across the Atlantic. There were some English boys in the crew, and one American boy. He was Joseph M. Meany, Jr., seventeen, of Waltham, Massachusetts. He had been chosen to make the trip after winning the Junior Citizenship Award of the Boys' Clubs of America.

On Thanksgiving Day, 1957, the ship was given to the United States. Today it is anchored in Plymouth Harbor where the first *Mayflower* landed. More than half a million visitors come every year to see the *Mayflower II*. Many also visit a model of the Pilgrims' first village nearby.

In Pilgrim Village, the guides are dressed like the early settlers. They show visitors through the houses and tell how the Pilgrims lived. On Thanksgiving Day, people of the town of Plymouth dress up as Pilgrims. They act out scenes in the lives of the early settlers.

In Plymouth there are statues and monuments to the Pilgrims. There is also a museum called Pilgrim Hall. Here you will find some of the Pilgrims' furniture. There is a cradle used by the first white child born in Massachusetts.

On the beach, Plymouth Rock marks the Pilgrims' landing place. It is protected now by stone pillars, a roof, and a strong iron fence. Otherwise, visitors might carry away bits of it as souvenirs. We would lose one of the most famous landmarks in America.

Thirty miles from Plymouth, across Cape Cod Bay, is Provincetown. People in Provincetown are quick to tell you that the Pilgrims landed there *first*. A stone marks the place.

It was in Plymouth, though, that the Pilgrims settled. It was there that the first American Thanksgiving was held. The Pilgrims had no idea what an important holiday they started. Today, hundreds of years later, the people of America still celebrate Thanksgiving.

2

In Search
of a Home

The first *Mayflower* left Plymouth, England, on September 16, 1620. This was the third time she had set sail for America. On the first sailings, there were two ships—the *Mayflower* and a smaller ship called the *Speedwell*. The *Speedwell* leaked so badly that it was decided she could never last through the voyage. The ships returned to England.

Some of the passengers were afraid to

go on. The rest from the *Speedwell* crowded into the *Mayflower*. There were 102 people on the small ship—50 men, 20 women, and 32 children. Some of these were Pilgrims who were leaving England to find a place to worship God in their own way. In those days, everyone in England had to worship as the King wished.

The Pilgrims had moved to Holland for a time. In Holland they could worship as they pleased. But they found that their children were forgetting the English language and customs. In the New World they would be free to live as they wished and to start their own churches.

Not all the passengers on the *Mayflower* belonged to the Pilgrims' church. These others were going to the New World for different reasons. Many of them hoped to

make a better living in the new land. The Pilgrims called these people "strangers."

The largest family on board the *Mayflower* was that of Stephen Hopkins. Besides his wife there were fifteen-year-old Constance, thirteen-year-old Giles, and little Damaris, age three. Baby Hopkins was born during the voyage and was named Oceanus.

The most lively children aboard were probably the Billingtons. Francis and John were always getting into mischief. Francis almost blew up the *Mayflower* when he shot off a firecracker near some powder kegs.

Among the leaders of the Pilgrims were William Brewster, Edward Winslow, John Carver and William Bradford. Later William Bradford wrote about the voyage and the settlement.

A soldier, Captain Miles Standish, went along to protect the new colony. Miles Standish had red hair and a quick temper. Some called him "Captain Shrimp" because he was a little man. He was also called "a little chimney." When he grew angry it seemed as if he "smoked" and shot off sparks!

There were many fierce storms during the voyage. The *Mayflower* rolled and tossed and shook. During one storm, there was a fearful crack. The main beam in the middle of the ship had broken. Luckily, the crew was able to raise it again and brace it with heavy posts.

The Pilgrims usually ate cold food for the ship had no kitchen. There were lots of hard biscuits, dried cheese and salted meat. Sometimes the Pilgrims cooked over a little fire laid in a box of sand. This

13

could not be used in bad weather because of the danger of fire. Often the Pilgrims were too seasick to eat. The ship was small, crowded and uncomfortable. Some people had to sleep on deck in the ship's small boat.

The *Mayflower* sailed for 66 long days and nights. On November 20 land was sighted. What a welcome sight it was! The Captain said it was Cape Cod, New England. It had been named for the many codfish there. The little ship now headed south.

The Pilgrims were not the first English people to go to America. Fishermen had sailed along the coast for over 100 years. And in 1607 the first lasting English colony in the New World was begun at Jamestown, Virginia. At that time, "Virginia" stretched from Jamestown to

Maine. It was owned by England. The northern part was called North Virginia, or New England. The Pilgrims hoped to settle near the Hudson River.

The *Mayflower* sailed into very rough waters. The Captain decided to turn about. The ship struggled back to the tip of Cape Cod.

The next day, Saturday, November 21, they anchored in the harbor we now call

Provincetown. The deck was crowded. The children shouted excitedly.

The men decided it was too late and too dangerous to sail south again. Winter had begun. They would settle somewhere in this area.

Everyone was thankful that the hard voyage was over. The New England earth before them was a wilderness. It, too, was full of dangers. But at least these dangers were on dry land.

Before they went ashore, the men signed an agreement about their new government. This is now called the *Mayflower Compact*.

The compact promised just and equal laws for all. The men were given the right to choose their governor. Usually the King chose governors and other officers. The compact was the first example of democracy in the New World.

After the compact was signed, the people elected John Carver their first governor.

Now they had to find a place for their settlement. There was no time to be lost. It was getting colder every day.

Miles Standish led an armed exploring party of sixteen men. They saw a few Indians but the Indians ran away. The men tried to follow them, but lost them in the thick underbrush.

18

The next morning they found a spring of fresh water. How good it tasted after the stale water from the ship's barrels! This same spring can be seen today.

The men pushed on and found some deserted Indian cornfields. Hidden in piles of sand were baskets of seed corn, yellow and red mixed with blue. The Pilgrims had never seen this kind of grain. They hoped it would be good to plant. They took all they could carry. Later, when they found the Indians who had owned the corn, they paid them for it.

While the men were gone, one of the women on board ship, Mrs. William White, gave birth to a son. He was called Peregrine, which means Pilgrim or Wanderer. This was the first English child born in Massachusetts. It is his cradle that is in Pilgrim Hall today.

The explorers returned to the *Mayflower* without finding a good place to settle. The land was too low and sandy. The weather had turned very cold. They must search again and quickly for a place to spend the winter.

Now the exploring party started out in the ship's small sailboat. They would search the coast for a good harbor and high land. The winds were wild and it began to snow. First the boat's rudder broke. Then the mast snapped into three pieces. Somehow they reached a harbor safely.

The men rowed ashore to look over the land. There was a great rock at the water's edge where they landed. This is the famous rock we call Plymouth Rock.

Farther from shore they found a brook and some good high land. The land had

already been cleared for cornfields. That would make it easy for them to build homes. The Indians who had cleared the land were no longer about. But there were many Indian bones. The men decided that the Indians of the village must all be dead. It seemed to be a safe place for a settlement. Certainly it was the best one they had found so far.

They hurried back to the *Mayflower* with the heart-warming news. They had found a place to call "home."

3

The First Winter

Aboard the *Mayflower* the Pilgrims looked excitedly at a map of New England. It had been made by the explorer, Captain John Smith. Places along the coast had been given English names. The land the exploring party had chosen for their settlement was called Plymouth. This was also the name of the town they had sailed from in England.

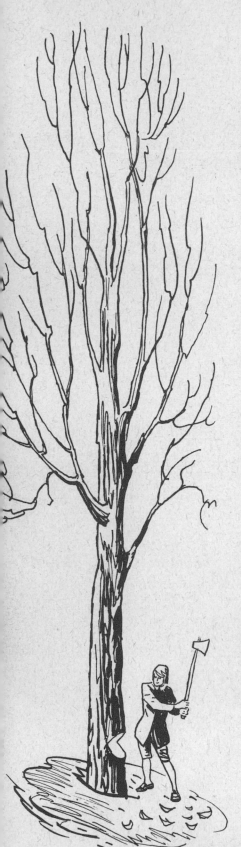

The *Mayflower* sailed into Plymouth harbor on December 26, 1620. It was a cold, icy day. But the people were happy to see their new home.

The men chose high ground above the brook for their houses. First of all, they needed to build a common house. It would serve as a storeroom and gathering place.

The men began to fell trees. Some chopped, some sawed logs for planks. It was heavy work. The cold New England weather did not make it easier. There was little snow that year, but it was very wet.

The women and small children stayed aboard ship. The older boys came ashore to help. They also did some exploring on their own.

Francis Billington climbed a tree one day. In wild excitement he shouted that

24

he saw a great sea. Perhaps it was the Pacific Ocean! What looked as big as an ocean to the boy turned out to be a large pond. The Pilgrims, who had little to laugh about, called it Billington's Sea. That is what it is called today.

There was little food left on the *Mayflower*. Some of the men went hunting. They had never hunted for food before. They made so much noise that most of the game got away.

There were plenty of fish in the bay. But the Pilgrims had not brought fishnets or hooks. They did gather clams and lobsters.

The winter wore on, long and terrible. Snow, sleet, or freezing rain stopped the work of building many times. The people were weak from cold and lack of food. Many became ill. Bradford called it the "Great Sickness."

Sometimes two or three people died in one day. Soon, out of more than 100 people, scarcely 50 remained alive. Of these only six or seven were well enough to help the others.

There were many secret graves on the hill overlooking the bay. The dead were buried at night. The settlers did not want any spying Indians to know how few of them were left alive.

Of eighteen married women, only five were left. The Pilgrim mothers had often gone without food to have more for their children. Some of the children died, but more were left orphans. The other people in the colony took them into their homes.

Luckily, spring came early the next year. In mid-March it was warm enough to plant gardens. The sick began to get well. At last the terrible winter was over.

4

Indian Visitors

During the winter the settlers had seen Indians, but only at a distance. When the Pilgrims tried to get near them, the Indians always ran away.

One day in March, a tall Indian walked boldly into the settlement. He was armed with a bow and arrows.

The children screamed. What would this savage do?

Suddenly the tall savage called out, "Welcome!" He spoke in English!

Surprised Pilgrims gathered about him. The Indian told them that his name was Samoset. He was a chief among his own people, 40 miles north. He had learned English from the fishermen along the coast.

Samoset told them the Indian name for Plymouth was Patuxet. Four years before, all the Indians there had died of a sickness. There was only one of their tribe left. His name was Squanto, and he had been to England. Samoset said he would bring Squanto to Plymouth.

Samoset also said there was a great chief named Massasoit who ruled nearby. Massasoit wished to speak with the Pilgrims. Squanto and Samoset would help them understand each other.

That night Samoset stayed with the

Hopkins family. Constance, Damaris and Giles probably found it hard to get to sleep. It was a fearsome thing to have a wild Indian in the house.

Samoset left Plymouth, happy with the gifts the Pilgrims had given him. A few days later he returned with Squanto.

Squanto told the Pilgrims he had been kidnapped by English shipmasters—twice! Friendly captains had returned him to his homeland.

When Chief Massasoit arrived, the settlers treated him with honor. His friendship was important to them. The leaders sat together on a green rug. They made a treaty of peace. This treaty was kept for 54 years.

Chief Massasoit and his men left. So did Samoset, but Squanto stayed. He told the Pilgrims he wanted to live with them.

5
The First Thanksgiving

Squanto became the best friend the Pilgrims had. Bradford said that he *"was a special instrument sent of God for their good."* Squanto stayed with the colony for the rest of his life.

He taught the Pilgrims how to catch fish and trap game. He showed them plants which they could use for medicine.

Most important, Squanto showed the Pilgrims how to plant Indian corn. The corn was put in hills of earth when the oak leaves were *"as big as a squirrel's ear."* Dead fish were put in the earth to make it rich.

Squanto planted other Indian vegetables, pumpkins and Indian beans. The English seeds, planted earlier, were already growing. The settlers looked forward hopefully to a good harvest. Without it they would surely starve during another winter in this new land.

In April the *Mayflower* sailed back to England. Now a good harvest was more important than ever. Not one of the Pilgrims went back with the ship. They knew there were more hardships ahead. But nothing could make them give up their new freedom of life.

33

During April Governor Carver died suddenly. The Pilgrims elected William Bradford as their new governor. Bradford was re-elected 30 times.

Summer was a busy time in the colony. The crops were gathered as they ripened. Wild berries were picked and dried.

The English wheat and peas did not do well. But the beans were a good crop. The Indian corn grew best of all.

The Pilgrims gathered in the harvest with thankful hearts. Almost everyone in the colony was in good health now. They had Squanto to help and guide them. They were at peace with the Indians.

On the hillside were seven snug little houses. They were made of wood planks with marsh grass thatch on the steep roofs. Each had a single room with a big fireplace. The children slept in a loft above.

There were also three storehouses and the common house. How much better all this was than the year before!

Governor Bradford thought that they should set aside a special day for thanksgiving. They decided to ask their Indian friends to celebrate with them. Squanto was sent to invite Chief Massasoit. This was probably sometime in October.

Four men went into the forest to hunt. They returned with many wild ducks, geese, turkeys and deer.

Giles Hopkins, the Billingtons and other boys gathered wood for the cooking fires. Most of the cooking was done outdoors.

Now the women began to prepare the food. The older girls helped, too. They made pies. They stuffed turkeys and geese with nuts. They prepared fish, eels, clams and oysters. They cooked corn bread and

roasted corn. Indian pudding, made of cornmeal and molasses, was boiled in bags.

Soon deer meat, turkeys and geese were turning on spits. Clam chowder and stews bubbled in pots hung over fires. Wonderful cooking smells filled the air.

On the morning of Thanksgiving Day, Massasoit marched out of the forest. With him were 90 braves!

The long line of Indians surprised the Pilgrims. They had not expected so many guests. But they gave no sign of their feelings. All of the Indians were made welcome.

Long tables were set up and the food was piled on them. The Indians ate and ate. They showed no sign of leaving. They were used to three- and four-day feasts.

Chief Massasoit knew that his braves were eating much of the Pilgrims' winter store of food. So he sent a hunting party into the forest. The braves returned with five deer. One was roasted whole for the feast. The others were a gift to the colony for later use.

While the women and girls got the next meal ready, and the next, the men played games. They ran races. They leaped and jumped.

Captain Miles Standish showed off his men. He marched them about. They fired their guns. They blew their bugles. The Indians were delighted. They showed their own skills with bows and arrows.

Massasoit and his braves stayed for three days. When they left, their friendship for the white people was stronger than ever. The first American Thanksgiving had been a great success.

6
Customs
Around
the World

In the United States we think of the Pilgrims' feast as the first Thanksgiving. Actually the custom of giving thanks for harvests, or other good fortune, goes back thousands of years.

One of the oldest known thanksgiving festivals goes back to the days before Christ. The Bible tells of the Hebrew Feast of the Tabernacles, or tents.

For seven days in the fall, the Hebrews lived in tents or in huts made from boughs. These were like the shelters the farmers used during the harvest in Palestine. The shelters were decorated with fruits, palm leaves and other branches. The people feasted and thanked God for the harvest.

The holiday was more than a harvest festival. It was also in memory of the Hebrews' forty-year search for the Promised Land. During their wanderings in the desert, the Hebrews had also lived in tents or tabernacles.

The festival is still celebrated by the Jewish people today, more than 3,000 years later. Sometimes it is called the Sukkoth. Now the Jewish people usually hang only boughs in their homes.

The ancient Greeks held two festivals a

year in honor of their harvest goddess, Demeter. They believed that Demeter's daughter, Persephone, was stolen by Pluto. He was the god of the Underworld. Demeter was very unhappy at the loss of her daughter. So she would not let anything grow in the upper world.

Persephone came home in the spring. Demeter, in her happiness, made the world bloom again. Grain sprouted in the fields. Fruit ripened on the vines.

However, Persephone was forced to return to the Underworld for six months every year. When this happened, winter came. Green things turned brown and seemed to die until the next spring.

One Greek festival in honor of Demeter came in September. It was so important that it was held even in wartime. The Greek states would stop fighting each other

to hold the festival. People marched in a long line with wreaths on their heads. They carried stalks of grain.

Another festival for Demeter was held in October at a temple near Athens. Only married women took part. On the first day they sang sad songs and went without food. This was in memory of Demeter's sorrow when her daughter disappeared. On the second day everything was gay and happy. This celebrated Persephone's return. The women feasted. Fruit and honey were offered the goddess to thank her for the good harvest.

The Romans took many of their holiday customs from the Greeks. They held their harvest festival in October also. It was called the Cerelia. It honored Ceres, the Roman goddess of grain and harvest. From Ceres, we get our word *cereal*.

There were parades, music, dancing and all kinds of sports. Of course there was a feast. A pig and the first cuttings of the harvest were offered to the goddess.

Good harvests have always been very important, and still are. They were even more important in early times when canning or freezing food was unknown. Then, when crops failed, starvation lay ahead. That is why a good harvest was a reason for celebration.

Harvesting was hard work. The crops had to be picked and stored quickly. Cold or rain might spoil them. Once the crops were safe, the people were ready for a holiday.

In England there were harvest festivals even in early times. Some of the customs came from the Romans, who conquered England in 55 B.C. In time, the harvest festival became known as "Harvest Home." People from a whole village came out to see the last wagon come in from the fields. The workers and their sweethearts followed the wagon, called the Hock Cart. They wore flowers and ribbons and sang as they walked.

A popular song was:
> "Harvest Home! Harvest Home!
> We've plowed, we've sowed,
> We've reaped, we've mowed,
> We've brought home every load,
> Hip, hip, hip, Harvest Home!"

In some villages, the last grain cut was decorated with ribbons and called the "Kern Doll." In other villages a pretty girl was chosen to be "Harvest Queen." She wore a wreath of cornflowers and golden stalks of grain.

The farm workers feasted together in a big barn or tent. Afterward there were games and dancing. At night everyone sang around huge bonfires.

Many other thanksgiving festivals are celebrated throughout the world. Not all of these are harvest festivals.

In China a festival of the Harvest

Moon has been celebrated for centuries. The moon is fullest on the fifteenth day of the eighth moon, or month. This day is known as the moon's birthday. The Chinese say that a rabbit lives on the moon and that they can see him when the moon is full. The women bake "moon cakes" with the figure of a rabbit on them.

There is another meaning to the moon cakes. Long ago China was invaded. Enemy soldiers lived in the people's homes. The Chinese leaders decided to kill the soldiers—all at once. How could they notify everyone of their plan?

Women were told to bake moon cakes. In each moon cake they hid a message, giving the time to strike. The plan worked and the enemy was destroyed. The Chinese people then celebrated the moon's birthday and their own freedom.

When the Pilgrims lived in Holland, they watched the Dutch people celebrate their freedom with a thanksgiving festival. Not long before, in 1574, Holland had been at war with Spain. The city of Leyden was attacked for more than a year. The people were starving.

Finally the Dutch cut the river dikes. When the Spaniards saw the water rising, they fled.

A Leyden boy crept outside the city walls. He found a pot of stew in a deserted Spanish camping place. He grabbed the pot and raced home. Soon afterward Dutch boats sailed up to the city. They brought bread and herring to the starving people.

Ever since, on the morning of October 3, bread and herring have been given free from the steps of Leyden City Hall. At supper every Leyden family has a pot of stew. In this way they celebrate the saving of their city. It is their own special thanksgiving.

Even in the New World, Indian tribes had thanksgiving feasts. The Iroquois held celebrations for the spirits of the strawberry, raspberry, bean and corn. Their final celebration included thanksgiving for all crops and prayers for future harvests.

Corn was the Indians' most important crop. All the tribes along the eastern seacoast held a Green Corn Dance. The feast lasted several days.

When the Pilgrims invited the Indians to their first Harvest Thanksgiving, the Redmen were not surprised. They, too, were used to celebrating harvest festivals.

7

We Give Thanks

There was no Thanksgiving festival in Plymouth in 1622. The Pilgrims' harvest was so poor there was nothing left over for a feast.

The winter was a hard one too. Spring finally came, but after planting time there was no rain. Day after day the hot sun beat down on the fields.

Governor Bradford ordered a day of fasting and prayer. The Pilgrims prayed together for nine hours. Suddenly clouds began to gather. The next morning rain fell on the dry fields. Soon all was green again. A special Thanksgiving Day was held July 30, 1623.

After this there were other harvest festivals, though not every year. New settlements were made and the custom spread. Each settlement set its own day.

The Thanksgiving food became more varied. Wild cranberries were picked in the bogs. Apples were gathered from the new trees brought over from England. The apples were made into cider and apple pies. Pumpkin and mince pies became popular too. Turkeys, which are native American birds, became the center of the Thanksgiving feast.

Families from near Plymouth moved to other colonies. They took the custom of Thanksgiving with them. But it was still a local holiday that varied from place to place. It was little known in the South.

In 1784, a special Thanksgiving was held when the American Revolution ended. Then in 1789, when the thirteen colonies had become the thirteen states, President George Washington called for a national Thanksgiving.

Washington made a proclamation setting the date, November 26. He said to thank God for the outcome of the war. The people were also to give thanks for their new government and for the freedom, safety and happiness which it made possible.

Later, President Madison proclaimed a Thanksgiving Day. This was at the end

of the War of 1812. It was the last nationwide Thanksgiving celebration for many years. Celebrations were still held but each state set its own day. Often the dates of the celebrations were different.

A New England lady, Mrs. Sarah Hale, felt Thanksgiving should be a day when everyone in the United States celebrated together. Mrs. Hale was a writer. In a book published in 1827 she said, *"Thanksgiving like the Fourth of July should be considered a national holiday and observed by all our people."*

Later, Mrs. Hale became the editor of a magazine called *Godey's Lady's Book.* She began to write articles about Thanksgiving. More than 150,000 women read what Sarah Hale had to say.

Mrs. Hale did not stop there. She wrote to important people asking them to help make Thanksgiving a national holiday. Finally President Lincoln invited Mrs. Hale to visit him.

President Lincoln liked Mrs. Hale's idea. In 1863, he proclaimed the last Thursday in November to be Thanksgiving Day. Since that time Thanksgiving has been celebrated every November. Ours is the first Thanksgiving in the world to be a legal, public, national holiday.

Thanksgiving became more and more popular. In the nineteenth century, when families were larger than they are today, Thanksgiving dinners were feasts for the whole family and relatives. Sometimes Thanksgiving visits stretched for days!

Today family gatherings may be smaller but that makes room for special guests. Newcomers and people without families are often invited to others' feasts. Thanksgiving is a day of sharing. Churches and charitable groups arrange Thanksgiving meals for the homeless and needy.

Whenever possible, the armed forces give their men turkey dinners. Soldiers and sailors pause for a harvest feast, even as the warring Greeks did centuries ago.

In 1939, President Franklin D. Roosevelt changed the date of Thanksgiving. Store-keepers wanted it to come earlier in

November, so there would be more time for Christmas shopping. The celebration was held earlier in the month for two years. But people did not like the idea. In 1941 Congress set the date as the fourth Thursday in November. That has been the day on which we celebrate Thanksgiving ever since.

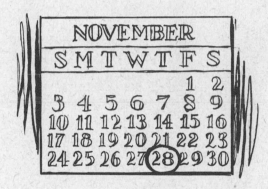

8
Thanksgiving Today

"Over the river and through the woods,
To Grandfather's house we go;
The horse knows the way
To carry the sleigh
Through the white and drifted snow . . ."

This Thanksgiving song-poem was written by Lydia Maria Child over 100 years ago. Thanksgiving had come to be a time of family gathering, as it still is today.

We may not go to Grandfather's house in a sleigh these days, but we try to visit our relatives by car, train or plane. It is a happy holiday that we like to enjoy with our families.

Of course, we always think of a big family dinner when we think of Thanksgiving. We feast on many of the same things the Pilgrims did: cranberries, corn, pumpkin and pies. Turkeys are placed proudly on the tables just as they were on the first Thanksgiving.

Thanksgiving afternoon, all over the United States, football games are played. In this way, too, we follow the Pilgrims' example. There were games and sports on the first Thanksgiving.

Thanksgiving Day is a serious day as well as a feast day. *"Come ye thankful people come"* is sung in churches and

schools throughout the country. We thank God for our blessings and for the privilege of living in the United States. We are especially thankful to the Pilgrims for their ideals of freedom and justice.

From earliest times people all over the world have found things to be thankful for. They have given thanks in their many different ways. Our American Thanksgiving was begun by the Pilgrims as thanks for a good harvest. It has come to mean much more than that. It is a day when each of us can count our blessings.